LET'S USE THE POTTY TOGETHER

Mastering Toilet Training with
Compassion and Care for Every Child

By Dasia Evans, PhD

Copyright @ 2024 Dasia Evans, PhD

Legal Notice

All rights reserved. No part of this book may be reproduced, stored in a retrieval system, or transmitted in any form or by any means, electronic, mechanical, photocopying, recording, or otherwise, without the prior written permission of the copyright owner, except for the use of brief quotations in a book review.

The author assumes no responsibility for any errors or omissions in the content of this book. Any references to specific products, services, or companies do not imply endorsement or suggestion.

Table of Contents

Overview of Potty Training 4
    An Understanding of the Process 4
    The Challenges of Potty Training 4
    Understanding Each Child's Unique Needs 6
Chapter 1 10
    Getting Ready for Potty Training 10
    Step 1: Recognizing Readiness Signs 10
    Step 2: Preparing Your Child 12
    Step 3: Preparing the Home Environment 13
    Step 4: Managing Accidents 14
    Step 5: Transitioning to Full Potty Training 15
Chapter 2 17
    Essential Potty Training Steps: A Comprehensive Guide 17
    Understanding Readiness 17
    Introducing the Potty 18
    Creating a Routine 18
    Teaching the Process 19
    Addressing Common Challenges 20
    Dealing with Resistance 21

Transitioning to Success 21

Chapter 3 23

Potty Training Techniques for Children with Special Needs 23

Understanding the Basics 23

Communication Strategies 24

Sensory Adaptations 25

Routine and Consistency 26

Handling Challenges 27

Engaging with Specialists 27

Chapter 4 29

Advanced Potty Training Techniques and Strategies 29

Positive Reinforcement 29

Handling Regressions 31

Nighttime Training 33

Chapter 5 36

Potty Training Strategies for Different Settings 36

Potty Training at Home 36

Potty Training at Daycare 37

Potty Training in Public Restrooms 39

General Tips for All Settings 40

Chapter 6 42
   Managing Potty Training Accidents and
   Addressing Emotional Responses 42
   Understanding Accidents and Emotional
   Responses 42

Chapter 7 49
   Potty Training: Expert Insights and Personal
   Stories 49
   Expert Insights 49
   Personal Stories 51

Chapter 8 55
   Useful Resources and Tools for Potty Training ..55
   Apps 55
   Support Groups 56
   Examples of Recommended Tools and How to
   Use Them 58

Chapter 9 60
   Summary of the Potty Training Process and Next
   Steps 60
   Key Points of Potty Training 60
   Next Steps for Maintaining Progress 62

Chapter 10 66

Appendices for Potty Training Support...............66
Daily Progress Record..66
Weekly Summary Journal....................................68
Reward Survey..69
Progress Reflection Journal.................................70
Potty Training Tips Recap 72
Example Stories of Success.................................73
Encouragement Notes..74

Overview of Potty Training

An Understanding of the Process

One of the most significant developmental achievements in a child's early years is learning to use the toilet, which is a big step toward independence. It's a process that offers parents the satisfaction of seeing their child accomplish something genuinely significant along with obstacles and rewards that try their forbearance and resiliency. Potty training can be a scary thought for a lot of parents, especially when they take into account every child's individual needs, including those of children with special needs. . This introduction aims to guide you through the basics of potty training, highlighting the emotional and mental preparation necessary to make this journey as smooth and successful as possible.

The Challenges of Potty Training

Potty training is rarely a straightforward process. It involves teaching a young child to recognize their body's signals, to respond appropriately, and to take on a new responsibility—one that, for a time, may seem overwhelming to them. For parents, this process requires patience, consistency, and a deep understanding of their child's individual readiness and temperament.

One of the most common challenges parents face is knowing when to start. Every child is different, and while some may show signs of readiness as early as 18 months, others may not be ready until they are closer to three years old. This can be particularly true for children with special needs, who may require more time and a different approach. For these children, physical readiness might come later, and they may need extra support to understand the process.

Another challenge is dealing with setbacks. Even after initial success, it's normal for children to have accidents. This can be frustrating, but it's important to remember that setbacks are a natural part of learning. Parents might also face resistance from their child, who may be fearful or simply not interested in the process. This resistance can be more pronounced in children with special needs, who might have difficulty with changes in routine or sensory issues that make the experience uncomfortable.

The Rewards of Potty Training

Despite these challenges, potty training offers immense rewards for both the child and the parents. For the child, mastering this skill is a huge confidence booster. It's a step toward independence that helps them feel proud of themselves and capable of taking on new challenges. This newfound independence can also lead to greater self-esteem and a sense of responsibility.

For parents, successfully potty training their child brings a sense of accomplishment and relief. It's a clear sign of their child's growth and development, and it often makes daily routines easier. No more changing diapers, no more constant worry about accidents—it's a liberating experience for the whole family.

<u>Understanding Each Child's Unique Needs</u>

One of the most important aspects of potty training is recognizing that every child is unique. What works for one child may not work for another, and this is especially true for children with special needs. Some children may learn best through visual cues, while others might need more verbal encouragement or physical assistance.

For children with special needs, it's crucial to tailor the approach to their specific challenges. This might involve breaking down the steps into smaller, more manageable tasks, using visual schedules or social stories to help them understand what's expected, or providing additional sensory support, such as using a soft toilet seat or allowing them to hold a comforting object during the process. Consistency is key, as many children with special needs thrive on routine and predictability.

It's also important to consider any physical challenges the child may face. Some children might have difficulty with the physical act of sitting on the toilet, while others may struggle with understanding the sensations that signal the need to go. In these cases, working closely with healthcare professionals can provide valuable strategies and tools to support the child's success.

Preparing Parents Mentally and Emotionally

Potty training is as much about preparing parents as it is about preparing the child. Before beginning the process, it's important for parents to be mentally and emotionally ready. This means understanding that potty training is not a race—there's no need to compare your child's progress to others. Every child moves at their own pace, and pushing them too soon can lead to frustration for both the child and the parents.

Parents should also be prepared for the emotional ups and downs of the process. There will be good days and bad days, moments of triumph and times of doubt. It's normal to feel frustrated, especially when progress seems slow. However, maintaining a calm and positive attitude can make a big difference in how your child responds. Remember, your child will pick up on your emotions, so staying patient and encouraging will help them feel more confident.

It's also helpful to set realistic expectations. A crucial developmental stage for your child is learning to use the potty. Whether it's the first time your child tells you they need to go or their first accident-free day, these moments are worth acknowledging and celebrating.

Setting the Tone for a Supportive and Informative Guide

This book is designed to be your companion on the potty training journey, offering practical advice, expert insights, and real-life stories from parents who have been through it all. It's a guide that recognizes the individuality of each child and the unique challenges that come with potty training, especially for children with special needs.

Throughout this book, you'll find tips and strategies that are flexible and adaptable to your child's specific needs. Whether you're dealing with a child who is eager to start or one who is resistant, whether your child is typically developing or has special needs, this guide aims to provide you with the tools and confidence you need to navigate the process successfully.

Remember, potty training is not just about teaching your child a new skill—it's about fostering their independence, building their confidence, and strengthening the bond between you and your child. With patience, understanding, and the right support, you can make this a positive and rewarding experience for both of you.

Remember that you have support as you go out on this adventure. Many parents have faced the same challenges and come out the other side with happy, confident children. This book is here to support you every step of the way, offering guidance, encouragement, and a wealth of knowledge to help you through the ups and downs of potty training. Let's get started.

Chapter 1
Getting Ready for Potty Training

A Comprehensive Guide

Preparing for potty training is an exciting milestone for both you and your child. It involves careful planning and setting up a positive environment to ensure a smooth transition. This guide will walk you through preparing both your child and your home for potty training, with practical tips and clear, step-by-step instructions.

Step 1: Recognizing Readiness Signs

Before starting potty training, it's essential to ensure that your child is ready. Children show readiness in various ways, and recognizing these signs can help you determine the right time to begin.

- **Physical Signs:**

  Stays Dry for Longer Periods: If your child can keep their diaper dry for two hours or more, they may be ready for potty training.

Regular Bowel Movements: Consistent bowel movements at specific times can indicate readiness.

Shows Interest in the Bathroom: If your child is curious about the toilet or wants to follow you to the bathroom, it's a good sign.

- **Behavioral Signs:**

Follows Simple Directions: Your child should be able to understand and follow simple instructions.

Shows Independence: If your child is willing to try doing things on their own, like dressing or undressing, they may be ready for potty training.

Expresses Discomfort with Wet Diapers: Complaints about wet or soiled diapers are a clear sign that your child is ready to use the toilet.

- **Emotional Signs:**
  - **Demonstrates a Desire to Be Independent:** If your child is eager to do things by themselves and seems interested in being more grown-up, they might be ready for potty training.
  - **Shows Interest in Using the Toilet:** Talking about or wanting to use the toilet like adults is a good indicator.

Step 2: Preparing Your Child

Once you've identified the readiness signs, the next step is to prepare your child for potty training. Here's how to approach it:

- **Introduce the Concept:**
  - This books about potty training to help your child understand the process in a fun and relatable way.
    - **Talk About the Potty:** Have open and positive conversations about using the toilet, making it seem like a natural part of daily life.
- **Choose the Right Equipment:**
  - **Potty Training Chair or Adapter:** Select a potty chair or an adapter that fits securely on your regular toilet. Involve your child in choosing the potty to make them more excited.
  - **Step Stool:** If using an adapter, a step stool can help your child reach the toilet comfortably.
- **Establish a Routine:**
  - **Set Regular Times:** Encourage your child to sit on the potty at regular intervals, such as after meals, before naps, and before bedtime.
  - **Create a Schedule:** Consistency is key. Establish a daily routine to help your

child get used to using the potty regularly.
- **Encourage Practice:**
  - **Allow Practice Time:** Give your child opportunities to practice sitting on the potty, even if they don't always use it.
  - **Celebrate Efforts:** Praise your child for their attempts, regardless of the outcome, to build their confidence and enthusiasm.

Step 3: Preparing the Home Environment

Creating a conducive environment at home can significantly impact the success of potty training. Here's just how to organize your home:

- **Designate a Potty Area:**
  - **Choose a Convenient Location:** Place the potty in a location that is easily accessible for your child, such as a bathroom or a designated potty area.
  - **Ensure Privacy:** If possible, ensure that the potty area provides some privacy, as this can make your child more comfortable.
- **Stock Up on Supplies:**

- o **Training Pants:** Have training pants available as a transition between diapers and underwear.
  - o **Cleaning Supplies:** Keep cleaning supplies, such as disinfectant wipes and paper towels, handy for any accidents.
- **Encourage Independence:**
  - o **Easy-to-Remove Clothing:** Dress your child in clothing that they can easily remove by themselves, like elastic-waist pants.
  - o **Potty Training Chart:** Use a potty training chart to track progress and reward successes. This visual aid can motivate your child and help them understand their progress.
- **Create a Positive Atmosphere:**
  - o **Avoid Pressure:** Ensure that potty training is a positive experience. Avoid pressuring your child or showing frustration.
  - o **Provide Praise and Encouragement:** Celebrate successes with praise and encouragement to make the experience enjoyable.

Step 4: Managing Accidents

Accidents are a natural part of potty training. Here's how to handle them calmly:

- **Stay Calm:** React calmly and avoid expressing frustration. Your child will learn that accidents are part of the process and not something to be upset about.
- **Encourage Cleanup:** Involve your child in the cleanup process to help them understand the consequences of accidents and encourage them to try again.
- **Reinforce Positive Behavior:** Focus on the positives and reinforce successful potty usage with praise and rewards.

Step 5: Transitioning to Full Potty Training

As your child becomes more comfortable with using the potty, you can gradually transition to full potty training:

- **Increase Independence:** Encourage your child to use the potty independently, while offering support as needed.
- **Introduce Underwear:** Once your child has consistently used the potty, transition from training pants to regular underwear.
- **Maintain Consistency:** Continue with regular potty times and praise to reinforce good habits.

Preparing for potty training involves understanding readiness signs, preparing your child, and setting up your home environment. By following these steps and creating a positive, supportive atmosphere, you can make the potty training process smoother and more successful for both you and your child. Remember, patience and encouragement are key as your child navigates this new milestone.

By adopting these strategies, you can confidently approach potty training, ensuring that it becomes a positive experience for everyone involved.

Chapter 2
Essential Potty Training Steps: A Comprehensive Guide

One of a child's developmental milestones is learning to use the potty. It marks a transition from diapers to using the toilet, and while it can be a challenging process, with the right approach, it can be made smoother for both parents and children. This guide outlines essential potty training steps, covering general methods applicable to all children, creating a routine, and addressing common challenges.

Understanding Readiness

Signs of Readiness

Make sure your youngster is ready before beginning potty training. Signs of readiness include:

- **Physical Readiness:** Your child should have regular bowel movements and dry periods lasting at least two hours.
- **Behavioral Readiness:** They may show interest in using the toilet or express discomfort with dirty diapers.

- **Communication Skills:** Your child should be able to understand simple instructions and communicate their needs.

1.2 Choosing the Right Time

Begin potty training when there are no major changes in your child's life, such as moving to a new house or the arrival of a sibling. Consistency is key, so select a time when you can focus on training.

Introducing the Potty

Choosing a Potty

Decide between a potty chair or a seat that fits onto the regular toilet. Allow your child to choose, as this can increase their interest and enthusiasm.

Making the Potty Appealing

Make the potty an inviting place by letting your child decorate it or choose a favorite color. Place it in a visible location to remind them to use it.

Creating a Routine

Establishing a Schedule

Consistency is crucial in potty training. Create a routine that includes:

- **Regular Bathroom Visits:** Take your child to the potty every 2-3 hours, and after meals or naps.
- **Encouraging Regularity:** Encourage them to sit on the potty at specific times each day, even if they don't need to go.

Positive Reinforcement

Encourage your child with praise and rewards. Positive reinforcement can include:

- **Verbal Praise:** Offer enthusiastic praise when your child uses the potty correctly.
- **Reward System:** Consider a sticker chart or small rewards to motivate your child.

<u>Teaching the Process</u>

Demonstrating Use

Show your child how to use the potty by demonstrating, if appropriate. Explain the steps clearly:

- **Sitting on the Potty:** Teach your child to sit comfortably on the potty, even if they don't need to go.
- **Wiping and Flushing:** Show them how to wipe properly and flush the toilet.

Encouraging Independence

As your child becomes more comfortable, encourage them to do more on their own. Allow them to:

- **Dress Themselves:** Teach them to pull down their pants and underwear.
- **Wash Hands:** Emphasize the importance of washing hands after using the potty.

Addressing Common Challenges

Handling Accidents

Accidents are a normal part of potty training. To handle them:

- **Stay Calm:** Avoid punishment. Reassure your youngster instead that mishaps do occur.
- **Encourage Cleanup:** Have your child help clean up, which reinforces the importance of using the potty.

Dealing with Resistance

If your child resists using the potty:

- **Be Patient:** Avoid pressuring your child. Take a rest, and if necessary, try again later.
- **Offer Choices:** Let your child choose their potty training supplies or choose when to use the potty.

Nighttime Training

Nighttime potty training often comes after daytime training. To manage this:

- **Limit Fluids:** Reduce drinks before bedtime to minimize accidents.
- **Use Training Pants:** Consider using training pants or a waterproof mattress cover.

Transitioning to Success

Celebrating Milestones

Celebrate each milestone to encourage your child. Praise them for:

- **Dry Nights:** Recognize progress in staying dry throughout the night.

- **Consistent Use:** Celebrate consistent potty use during the day.

Maintaining Consistency

Keep the routine consistent even after your child seems fully trained. This helps reinforce the behavior and ensures lasting success.

For your child, potty training is a crucial developmental stage.for your child. By understanding signs of readiness, introducing the potty, creating a consistent routine, teaching the process, addressing challenges, and celebrating milestones, you can make the process smoother and more successful. Patience, encouragement, and a positive attitude will help your child navigate this important transition with confidence.

Chapter 3
Potty Training Techniques for Children with Special Needs

Potty training can be a challenging process, and when a child has special needs such as autism spectrum disorders (ASD) or other specific requirements, it requires additional strategies and adaptations. Here's a comprehensive guide to help you navigate potty training for children with special needs, focusing on communication and sensory issues, and offering practical tips for success.

Understanding the Basics

1. Assess Readiness Before starting potty training, it's crucial to assess if the child is ready. For children with ASD, signs of readiness may include:

- Staying dry for longer periods.
- Showing interest in using the toilet.
- Understanding simple instructions.

For other special needs, readiness might be determined by:

- The child's ability to follow routines.
- Awareness of bodily functions.

2. Set Realistic Goals Set small, achievable goals that can be gradually built upon. For example, start with short toilet visits and slowly increase the duration. Celebrate each success to build the child's confidence and motivation.

Communication Strategies

1. Use Visual Supports Children with autism often respond well to visual aids. Create a visual schedule that outlines the potty training routine. This can include:

- Pictures of the potty routine (e.g., washing hands, flushing, pulling up pants).
- A visual timer that indicates when it's time to use the toilet.

Example: Create a chart with images showing each step: walking to the toilet, sitting down, wiping, and flushing.

2. Simplify Language Use clear, simple language when giving instructions. Instead of saying, "It's time to go potty," you might say, "Time to sit on the potty."

Example: Use phrases like "Potty time" or "Sit down" and accompany them with gestures or signs.

3. Teach Through Modeling Demonstrate the potty routine for the child. This could involve using a doll or toy to show how to use the toilet. This hands-on approach helps children with ASD understand the process through observation.

Example: Use a favorite doll to model the steps of using the toilet and encourage the child to mimic the actions.

<u>Sensory Adaptations</u>

1. Address Sensory Sensitivities Children with autism might be sensitive to the sensory aspects of potty training. Consider the following adaptations:

- **Toilet Seat:** Use a cushioned or padded toilet seat if the child is uncomfortable with the standard seat.
- **Lighting:** Ensure the bathroom lighting is soft if bright lights are overwhelming.
- **Sound:** The sound of flushing can be startling. Allow the child to get used to the sound by flushing the toilet when the child is not in the room initially.
- **Example:** Provide noise-canceling headphones if the flushing sound is too loud for the child.

2. Choose Comfortable Clothing Select clothing that is easy to remove. Avoid clothes with complicated fastenings or tags that might irritate the child. Elastic-waist pants or leggings can be more comfortable and manageable.

Example: Opt for pants with elastic waistbands that the child can easily pull down and up by themselves.

Routine and Consistency

1. Establish a Routine Children with special needs often thrive on routine. Create a consistent potty training schedule. For example, have the child sit on the potty after meals, before naps, and before bedtime.

Example: Set a timer to remind you to take the child to the toilet at regular intervals, such as every two hours.

2. Use Positive Reinforcement Encourage and motivate the child with positive reinforcement. Praise, stickers, or small rewards can help reinforce the behavior. Make sure the child understands the purpose of the rewards.

Example: Create a reward chart where the child earns a sticker each time they successfully use the toilet.

Handling Challenges

1. Addressing Resistance If the child shows resistance or anxiety about using the toilet, don't force them. Instead, address their concerns and gradually introduce the potty in a low-pressure way.

Example: Allow the child to explore the potty at their own pace, letting them sit on it fully clothed before moving on to using it with pants down.

2. Managing Accidents Accidents are a normal part of the potty training process. Approach them with patience and without punishment. Use accidents as learning opportunities to reinforce the importance of using the toilet.

Example: If an accident occurs, calmly clean up and remind the child of the next step in the routine.

Engaging with Specialists

1. Seek Professional Advice Engage with therapists or specialists who have experience working with children with special needs. They can provide tailored strategies and support specific to the child's needs.

Example: Consult with an occupational therapist who can offer additional sensory integration techniques.

2. Collaborate with Educators If the child is in school or daycare, work with their educators to ensure consistency between home and educational settings. Discuss plans of actions and advancement to forge cohesive strategies

Example: Provide the child's teacher with the visual schedule and potty training goals so they can reinforce the routine during school hours.

Potty training for children with special needs requires patience, flexibility, and understanding. By using visual supports, simplifying communication, addressing sensory issues, and maintaining a consistent routine, you can make the process smoother and more successful. Remember to celebrate progress, seek support when needed, and adapt strategies to fit the child's unique needs.

With these strategies, you can navigate the challenges of potty training with confidence and help your child achieve success.

Chapter 4
Advanced Potty Training Techniques and Strategies

Introduction

Potty training can be a complex process, and while basic techniques can get you started, advanced strategies often make the journey smoother and more successful. This guide provides detailed methods for advanced potty training, focusing on positive reinforcement, handling regressions, and nighttime training. Each section includes practical tips, effective rewards, and troubleshooting advice to support a successful potty training experience.

Positive Reinforcement

Overview

Positive reinforcement is a technique that encourages desired behavior by offering rewards or praise. It helps children feel motivated and proud of their progress, making them more likely to repeat the desired behavior.

Techniques

1. **Immediate Praise and Rewards**
   - **Description:** Give immediate praise or a small reward each time your child successfully uses the potty.
   - **Example:** If your child successfully uses the potty, offer a sticker or verbal praise right away. This immediate feedback helps them connect their action with the reward.
   - **Tip:** Use enthusiastic and specific praise like, "Great job staying dry and using the potty!"
2. **Reward Charts**
   - **Description:** Create a reward chart to visually track your child's progress and motivate them.
   - **Example:** Design a chart where your child earns a sticker for each successful potty use. After accumulating a certain number of stickers, they can choose a small prize.
   - **Tip:** Make the chart colorful and place it in a visible area to remind and motivate your child.
3. **Token Systems**
   - **Description:** Implement a token system where your child earns tokens for each successful potty use, which can be exchanged for a larger reward.
   - **Example:** Your child earns one token for each successful potty visit. After collecting ten tokens, they can exchange them for a favorite toy or activity.

- **Tip:** Ensure the rewards are meaningful and desirable to your child.

Troubleshooting Tips

- **Inconsistent Rewards:** Ensure that rewards are given consistently to maintain motivation. Inconsistencies can lead to confusion and reduced effectiveness.
- **Over-reliance on Rewards:** Gradually phase out rewards as your child becomes more comfortable with potty use to encourage intrinsic motivation.

Handling Regressions

Overview

Regressions can occur when a child temporarily returns to old habits, such as accidents after a period of successful potty use. Understanding and managing regressions is crucial to maintaining progress.

Techniques

1. **Identify Triggers**
    - **Description:** Determine if there are specific factors contributing to the regression, such as stress, illness, or changes in routine.

- **Example:** If your child has been having accidents after starting daycare, consider if the new environment or changes in routine might be causing stress.
- **Tip:** Keep a diary of incidents to identify patterns or triggers.

2. **Maintain Consistency**
   - **Description:** Continue using the established potty training routine even during periods of regression.
   - **Example:** Stick to regular potty times and continue offering praise and rewards to reinforce the behavior.
   - **Tip:** Avoid expressing frustration or anger; instead, calmly remind your child of the expectations.

3. **Reassess Readiness**
   - **Description:** Evaluate if your child might need additional support or if there might be a need to adjust the training approach.
   - **Example:** If regressions persist, consider if your child might not be fully ready for training and if a break might be beneficial.
   - **Tip:** Be patient and flexible with the training process.

Troubleshooting Tips

- **Overreacting to Accidents:** Avoid making a big deal out of accidents, as this can increase anxiety and exacerbate regressions.
- **Inconsistent Routine:** Ensure that the potty training routine is consistent across all environments (home, daycare, etc.).

Nighttime Training

Overview

Nighttime potty training can be challenging because it involves helping your child stay dry overnight. This often requires different strategies than daytime training.

Techniques

1. **Establish a Bedtime Routine**
    - **Description:** Create a consistent bedtime routine that includes using the potty right before bed.
    - **Example:** Ensure your child uses the potty right before getting into bed and limit fluid intake in the evening.
    - **Tip:** Avoid giving drinks close to bedtime to reduce the likelihood of nighttime accidents.
2. **Use Protective Bedding**

- **Description:** Use waterproof mattress protectors and training pants to manage accidents and provide reassurance.
- **Example:** Place a waterproof cover on the mattress and consider using pull-ups or bedwetting pants as a temporary measure.
- **Tip:** Choose bedding that is easy to clean and comfortable for your child.
3. Encourage Nighttime Potty Visits
    - **Description:** If your child wakes up during the night, encourage them to use the potty if they feel the urge.
    - **Example:** Leave a nightlight on in the bathroom and guide your child to use the potty if they wake up wet.
    - **Tip:** Make nighttime potty visits as quick and easy as possible to avoid waking your child too much.

Troubleshooting Tips

- **Early Success vs. Ongoing Accidents:** If your child initially succeeds but later experiences accidents, reassess fluid intake and bedtime routines.
- **Bedwetting and Medical Concerns:** If nighttime accidents persist beyond the typical age for training, consider consulting a healthcare professional to rule out any underlying issues.

Advanced potty training techniques, including positive reinforcement, handling regressions, and nighttime training, can significantly improve the potty training experience for both parents and children. By implementing these strategies thoughtfully and maintaining consistency, you can support your child's journey toward successful and independent potty use. Use the provided examples and troubleshooting tips to address common challenges and foster a positive training environment.

Chapter 5
Potty Training Strategies for Different Settings

As an early childhood educator, understanding how to navigate potty training across various settings is essential for ensuring a smooth and successful process. Potty training can be challenging, but with the right strategies tailored to home, daycare, and public restrooms, it becomes manageable. Here's a comprehensive guide to help parents and caregivers adapt potty training techniques to each setting.

Potty Training at Home

Creating a Consistent Routine

- **Set Regular Times:** Establish a potty schedule that aligns with your child's natural bathroom habits. This can include after meals, naps, and before bed. Consistency helps reinforce the routine and encourages regular bathroom use.
- **Use Visual Cues:** Consider using a visual schedule or a potty chart to help your child understand when it's time to use the potty. Visual aids can provide a sense of structure and predictability.

Making the Bathroom Child-Friendly

- **Size-Appropriate Equipment:** Invest in a potty that suits your child's size, or use a potty seat that fits securely on the regular toilet. Ensure that your child can comfortably reach the seat and the toilet paper.
- **Encourage Independence:** Teach your child how to pull down their pants, wipe properly, and wash their hands. Make sure these steps are part of the routine to build their confidence and independence.

Handling Accidents with Patience

- **Stay Calm:** Accidents are a natural part of potty training React coolly and tell your kid it's alright.
- Avoid punishment, as it can create negative associations with potty training.
- **Teach Problem-Solving:** Use accidents as an opportunity to discuss what went wrong and how to improve. For instance, if your child had an accident because they were too busy playing, remind them to listen to their body's signals.

Potty Training at Daycare

Communicating with Caregivers

- **Share Potty Training Goals:** Ensure that daycare staff are informed about your child's potty training goals,

schedule, and any specific needs. Success in daycare depends on home and daycare being consistent.
- **Provide Supplies:** Send your child with extra clothes and any specific potty training supplies they might need, such as a portable potty seat or wipes.

Establishing a Routine

- **Synchronize Schedules:** Work with daycare providers to synchronize potty breaks with your home routine. This ensures that your child receives consistent prompts and reinforcement throughout the day.
- **Encourage Positive Reinforcement:** If the daycare has a reward system, make sure it aligns with your home rewards. This helps reinforce the behavior and creates a sense of continuity.

Dealing with Daycare-Specific Challenges

- **Addressing Peer Influence:** Children may feel pressure or distraction from their peers. Encourage the daycare staff to offer positive reinforcement and create a supportive environment for all children involved in potty training.
- **Handling Disruptions:** Be prepared for potential disruptions, such as changes in staff or schedules. Communicate openly with the daycare to address any issues promptly and ensure your child's needs are met.

Potty Training in Public Restrooms

Preparing Your Child

- **Familiarize with Public Restrooms:** Before venturing out, let your child explore a public restroom to get accustomed to the setting. Explain the differences from their home bathroom and how to use it confidently.
- **Practice Good Hygiene:** Teach your child how to use public restrooms hygienically. Explain the importance of washing hands thoroughly and using toilet paper properly.

Using Portable Solutions

- **Carry a Portable Potty Seat:** If your child is uncomfortable using public toilets, consider carrying a portable potty seat. This can provide a familiar and comfortable experience, making the transition easier.
- **Bring Hygiene Supplies:** Pack essential items like hand sanitizer, wipes, and extra clothing. This ensures you are prepared for any situation and helps maintain hygiene.

Addressing Common Concerns

- **Overcoming Fear:** Public restrooms can be intimidating for young children. Reassure them that

it's a normal part of being out and that they can always ask for help if needed.
- **Managing Emergencies:** In case of an urgent need, be prepared to act quickly. If a public restroom is unavailable, find the nearest facility or consider carrying a small, emergency travel potty.

General Tips for All Settings

Consistency is Key

- **Stick to the Routine:** Consistency across home, daycare, and public settings helps reinforce potty training. Ensure that your child receives the same cues, encouragement, and routines wherever they are.

Positive Reinforcement

- **Celebrate Successes:** Use praise and rewards to celebrate successful potty trips. This reinforces positive behavior and motivates your child to continue using the potty regularly.

Patience and Flexibility

- **Adapt as Needed:** Be flexible and adapt your strategies as your child progresses through potty training. Every child is different, and it's important to adjust your approach based on their individual needs and responses.

Open Communication

- **Discuss Potty Training:** Regularly talk with your child about potty training and listen to their feelings. Address any concerns or fears they may have and provide reassurance and encouragement.
-

By applying these strategies in home, daycare, and public restroom settings, you can create a supportive and consistent potty training experience for your child. Understanding and adapting to each setting's unique challenges ensures a smoother transition and helps build your child's confidence and independence in their potty training journey.

Chapter 6
Managing Potty Training Accidents and Addressing Emotional Responses

Introduction

For both parents and children, potty training may be a difficult time. Accidents are a normal part of the process, and how you handle them can make a significant difference in your child's experience. This guide offers practical tips for managing potty training accidents and addressing emotional responses while maintaining a positive approach. By understanding and addressing these challenges, you can help your child succeed in their potty training journey.

Understanding Accidents and Emotional Responses

Accidents are an inevitable part of potty training. Children are learning to control their bladders and bowels, and this can take time. When accidents occur, it's crucial to approach the situation calmly and constructively. Children may feel embarrassed, frustrated, or even scared after an accident, and how you respond can impact their confidence and progress.

1. Stay Calm and Positive

Actionable Tip: Your reaction to an accident sets the tone for how your child will handle it. If you react with frustration or anger, your child may become anxious about using the toilet. Instead, stay calm and positive Assure your child that mishaps happen often and are a necessary part of learning.

Example: Say something like, "It's okay, accidents happen," if your youngster has an accident. Let's tidy up and give it another go later."

2. Reinforce Positive Behavior

Actionable Tip: Focus on and praise your child's successes. Positive reinforcement encourages them to continue using the potty and builds their confidence.

Example: When your child successfully uses the toilet, celebrate the achievement. You might say, "Great job using the potty! I'm so proud of you."

3. Establish a Routine

Actionable Tip: Create a consistent potty routine to help your child understand when and where they should use the toilet. Consistency can help reduce the frequency of accidents.

Example: Establish regular times for potty breaks, such as after meals, before naps, and before bedtime. Use a timer or an alarm to remind your child when it's time to try using the potty.

4. Use Positive Reinforcement

Actionable Tip: Implement a reward system to motivate your child. Rewards can be stickers, small treats, or extra playtime. Make sure your kid will find the rewards meaningful.

Example: Create a sticker chart where your child earns a sticker for each successful potty use. After collecting a certain number of stickers, they can choose a small reward.

5. Addressing Refusal and Resistance

Actionable Tip: If your child resists using the potty, it's essential to understand the underlying reasons. They might be uncomfortable with the potty, or they might be feeling pressured.

Example: If your child refuses to use the potty, try to identify the issue. It could be that the potty is uncomfortable or that they are afraid of flushing. Address these concerns by making the potty more inviting or explaining the flushing process in a calm manner.

6. Provide Reassurance and Support

Actionable Tip: Offer comfort and reassurance to help your child overcome fears or anxiety related to potty training. Make sure they feel supported and encouraged throughout the process.

Example: If your child is afraid of the sound of flushing, let them know that it's a normal sound and doesn't hurt. You can also practice flushing with them in a positive and relaxed setting.

7. Encourage Independence

Actionable Tip: Help your child become more independent in their potty training by teaching them how to manage their own hygiene. This includes wiping properly and washing their hands.

Example: Demonstrate proper wiping techniques and explain the importance of handwashing after using the toilet. Encourage your child to practice these skills with your guidance.

8. Create a Potty Training Kit

Actionable Tip: Assemble a potty training kit with essentials that your child can access easily. This can include wipes, a spare change of clothes, and a small bag for dirty clothes.

Example: Keep the kit in a convenient location where your child can reach it if they have an accident. This helps them feel more in control and prepared for accidents.

9. Practice Patience

Actionable Tip: Remember that potty training is a gradual process and requires patience. Children may have setbacks, and it's important to be understanding and supportive.

Example: If your child has frequent accidents, remind yourself that this is part of the learning process. Avoid expressing frustration and instead focus on providing encouragement and support.

10. Addressing Nighttime Training

Actionable Tip: Nighttime potty training can take longer than daytime training. Consider using training pants or waterproof bed covers to manage nighttime accidents.

Example: If your child has nighttime accidents, reassure them that this is normal. Gradually reduce the use of training pants as they show signs of staying dry through the night.

11. Involve Your Child in the Process

Actionable Tip: Involve your child in the potty training process to make them feel more invested. Let them choose their potty, pick out training pants, or select a potty training book.

Example: Take your child shopping for a potty or let them choose a fun potty training book. This involvement can make the process more engaging and less stressful for them.

12. Seek Professional Advice if Needed

Actionable Tip: If you encounter persistent issues or challenges with potty training, consider seeking advice from a pediatrician or child psychologist. They are able to offer advice based on your child's need.

Example: If your child continues to have frequent accidents or shows extreme resistance to potty training, consult a professional for additional support and strategies.

Managing potty training accidents and addressing emotional responses requires a combination of patience, positivity, and practical strategies. By staying calm, reinforcing positive behavior, and providing consistent support, you can help your child navigate this important developmental milestone with confidence and ease. Remember, every child is different, and it's important to adapt your approach to fit your child's unique needs and personality. With time and understanding, your child will gain the skills they need to succeed in potty training.

Chapter 7
Potty Training: Expert Insights and Personal Stories

Potty training is a significant step in every child's development, and for many parents, it can also be a challenging journey. To offer a comprehensive view of this important process, we've gathered expert insights and real-life stories from parents who have navigated the world of potty training. Through interviews with specialists and personal anecdotes, we aim to provide a well-rounded perspective on what works, what doesn't, and how to approach potty training with confidence.

Expert Insights

1. Understanding Readiness

Dr. Emily Carter, a pediatrician with over 20 years of experience, emphasizes the importance of recognizing a child's readiness for potty training. "Every child is unique," Dr. Carter explains. "There's no one-size-fits-all approach. It's crucial to look for signs that your child is physically and emotionally prepared."

Dr. Carter highlights several key readiness indicators:

- **Physical Signs:** Staying dry for longer periods, showing discomfort with dirty diapers.
- **Emotional Signs:** Expressing interest in using the toilet, understanding simple instructions.

She advises parents to avoid starting potty training too early, as this can lead to frustration for both the child and the parent. "It is preferable to hold off until the child expresses interest and readiness. This guarantees a more seamless shift and reduced anxiety for all parties concerned."

2. The Power of Positive Reinforcement

According to Dr. Karen Liu, a child psychologist specializing in behavioral development, positive reinforcement is a powerful tool in potty training. "Children respond well to encouragement and rewards. It's critical to recognize and honor their accomplishments, no matter how modest."

Dr. Liu suggests:

- **Praise and Rewards:** Offer verbal praise and small rewards for successful attempts. Stickers or extra storytime can be effective incentives.
- **Consistency:** Maintain a consistent approach to reinforcement. This helps children understand the

connection between their actions and the positive outcomes.

Dr. Liu cautions against punishment for accidents. "Potty training is a learning process. Reactions that are negative might impede growth and cause worry."

3. Tailoring Techniques to Individual Needs

Behavioral therapist Alex Johnson highlights the importance of tailoring potty training techniques to fit each child's needs. "Some children might respond better to visual aids, while others might benefit from a more structured routine."

Johnson recommends:

- **Visual Schedules:** Use charts with pictures to outline the potty routine. This can be especially helpful for children with autism or other developmental differences.
- **Routine Establishment:** Create a consistent schedule for potty breaks. This helps children learn when to expect bathroom visits and reinforces the routine.

Personal Stories

1. Sarah's Journey: From Diapers to Success

Sarah, a mother of two, shares her experience with potty training her first child, Emma. "Emma was a bit resistant at first. She didn't show much interest, and we were struggling to get her to use the potty regularly."

Sarah decided to try a more gradual approach. "We started by letting Emma pick out her own potty training supplies. She chose a fun, colorful potty and matching training pants. It made her excited about the process."

Sarah also used positive reinforcement, offering Emma small rewards like stickers for successful attempts. "It was incredible to witness the increase in her motivation.". She felt proud of her achievements, and that made a huge difference."

Emma eventually mastered potty training, and Sarah's approach of making it enjoyable and rewarding played a crucial role in their success.

2. James and Laura's Adaptation: Potty Training with Autism

James and Laura faced unique challenges potty training their son, Noah, who is on the autism spectrum. "Noah struggled with transitions and had difficulty understanding the concept of potty training," James explains.

Laura worked closely with their pediatrician to develop a tailored strategy. "We employed a regular schedule in addition to visual assistance. Noah's potty training chart had pictures of each step, from pulling down his pants to flushing the toilet."

They also incorporated Noah's interests into the process. "Noah loves trains, so we used train-themed rewards and created a train-themed potty training game. This made the whole experience more engaging for him."

Through patience and adaptation, James and Laura were able to help Noah make significant progress in his potty training journey.

3. Emma's Story: A Positive Approach to Nighttime Training

Emma, a mother of three, shares her approach to nighttime potty training. "My youngest, Liam, was a bit older than my other two when we started nighttime training. We knew he was ready, but we were unsure how to approach it."

Emma followed a gradual approach to nighttime training. "We started by limiting Liam's fluids in the evening and using a training potty in his room. We also made sure he went to the bathroom before bed."

She highlights the importance of patience and reassurance. "There were accidents, but we stayed positive and avoided making a big deal out of them. Encouragement and reassurance helped Liam feel more confident."

Emma's positive approach and gradual transition helped Liam successfully achieve nighttime potty training.

Potty training is a multifaceted process that can vary greatly from child to child. Expert insights from professionals like Dr. Carter, Dr. Liu, and Alex Johnson provide valuable guidance on recognizing readiness, using positive reinforcement, and tailoring techniques to individual needs. Meanwhile, personal stories from parents like Sarah, James, Laura, and Emma illustrate the practical applications of these strategies and the real-life challenges and triumphs of potty training.

Whether you are starting the journey with your child or facing specific challenges, these insights and stories can offer support and inspiration. Remember, patience and consistency are key, and every child's path to mastering potty training is unique

Chapter 8

Useful Resources and Tools for Potty Training

Potty training can be a challenging process, but having the right resources and tools can make it easier and more effective. This guide lists and describes useful resources, including books, apps, and support groups, that can help parents and caregivers navigate potty training successfully.

Apps

Apps can provide interactive support, reminders, and tracking tools to make potty training engaging and organized.

1. **Potty Training Timer**
    - **Description:** This app helps parents set reminders for potty breaks and track progress. It offers customizable schedules based on the child's needs and habits.
    - **How to Use:** Set up reminders for regular potty breaks and use the tracking feature to monitor your child's success rate. The app can also help

identify patterns and adjust the training schedule as needed.
2. **iPotty Training**
    - **Description:** iPotty Training provides a range of games and activities designed to make potty training fun. It includes visual rewards and progress tracking.
    - **How to Use:** Engage your child with the app's interactive games that are designed to reinforce potty training concepts. Use the progress tracking feature to celebrate milestones and keep your child motivated.
3. **Potty Time with Elmo**
    - **Description:** This app, featuring Elmo from Sesame Street, combines potty training lessons with entertaining activities. It uses familiar characters to encourage and educate children about potty training.
    - **How to Use:** Incorporate the app into your child's routine by letting them use it during designated potty times. The app's engaging content can help reinforce the potty training process in a fun way.

Support Groups

Support groups offer emotional support, advice, and shared experiences from other parents and caregivers.

1. **Online Forums (e.g., BabyCenter, What to Expect)**
    - o **Description:** These forums provide a platform for parents to ask questions, share experiences, and get advice from other families who have gone through potty training.
    - o **How to Use:** Join relevant discussions or start your own thread to get advice on specific issues. Engaging with the community can provide new insights and support during the potty training journey.
2. **Facebook Groups (e.g., Potty Training Support)**
    - o **Description:** Facebook groups dedicated to potty training offer a space for parents to connect, share tips, and seek encouragement. These groups often feature a variety of perspectives and solutions.
    - o **How to Use:** Join the group and participate in discussions. Share your experiences and ask questions to get advice tailored to your situation. The group can also offer motivation and reassurance.
3. **Local Parenting Groups and Classes**
    - o **Description:** Many communities offer parenting groups or classes focused on potty training. These can provide hands-on support and the opportunity to learn from professionals and other parents.

- **How to Use:** Check local community centers, hospitals, or parenting organizations for available classes or support groups. Attending these can offer personalized guidance and the chance to discuss concerns with experts.

Examples of Recommended Tools and How to Use Them

1. **Potty Training Charts**
   - **Description:** Charts help track your child's progress and reward successes. They can be a motivational tool that visually represents achievements.
   - **How to Use:** Create or purchase a chart and use stickers or markers to record each successful potty visit. Set up a reward system to encourage consistency and celebrate milestones.
2. **Training Potties and Seats**
   - **Description:** Training potties and seat inserts are essential tools for potty training. They come in various designs to suit different needs and preferences.
   - **How to Use:** Choose a training potty or seat that your child finds comfortable and easy to use. Encourage them to use it

regularly and incorporate it into their daily routine.

By utilizing these resources and tools, you can make the potty training process smoother and more successful. Each tool and resource provides unique benefits, from structured guidance in books to interactive support through apps and community advice from support groups. Incorporate these tools into your potty training plan to address various challenges and celebrate your child's progress.

Chapter 9
Summary of the Potty Training Process and Next Steps

Potty training is a significant milestone for both children and parents. It involves teaching your child to use the toilet instead of diapers. Here's a clear summary of the key points in the potty training process, along with suggestions for maintaining progress and celebrating successes.

Key Points of Potty Training

1. **Preparation and Readiness**
   - **Signs of Readiness:** Look for signs that your child is ready to start potty training, such as showing interest in using the toilet, staying dry for longer periods, and understanding basic instructions.
   - **Gather Supplies:** Prepare essential items like a child-sized potty or a seat adapter for the regular toilet, training pants, and easy-to-remove clothing.
2. **Establishing a Routine**
   - **Consistency is Key:** Create a regular schedule for potty breaks. Encourage your child to sit on the potty at regular

intervals, such as after meals, before naps, and before bed.
- **Encouragement and Praise:** Use positive reinforcement to encourage your child. Praise them when they successfully use the potty, and celebrate their achievements with stickers or extra playtime.

3. **Teaching the Process**
    - **Demonstrate and Explain:** Show your child how to use the potty. Explain the process in simple terms and use clear, consistent language.
    - **Practice Good Hygiene:** Teach your child how to wipe properly and wash their hands after using the toilet.

4. **Handling Accidents**

- **Stay Calm and Supportive:** Accidents are a normal part of potty training. Avoid scolding your child Reassure them instead, and urge them to give it another go.
- **Learn from Mistakes:** Use accidents as learning opportunities. If an accident happens, discuss what could be done differently and how to recognize the need to use the potty.

5. **Nighttime Training**
    - **Prepare for Nighttime:** Nighttime potty training may take longer. Ensure your

child uses the potty before bed and consider using training pants at night.
- **Gradual Transition:** Transition from nighttime training pants to underwear when your child consistently stays dry through the night.

Next Steps for Maintaining Progress

1. Reinforce the Routine
    - **Keep the Routine Consistent:** Maintain the potty training schedule even if your child experiences setbacks. Consistency helps reinforce the habit.
    - **Adjust as Needed:** Be flexible and adjust the routine if needed based on your child's progress and any changes in their schedule.
2. Celebrate Achievements
    - **Recognize Milestones:** Celebrate milestones, such as using the potty consistently or transitioning to underwear. Your child may be motivated by small prizes or unique activities.
    - **Positive Reinforcement:** Continue to provide praise and encouragement.

Celebrate their progress and reinforce their success with positive feedback.
3. **Monitor and Support**
    o **Observe and Support:** Pay attention to any signs of regression or issues that may arise. Offer support and reassurance as needed.
    o **Communicate with Caregivers:** If your child is in daycare or has other caregivers, ensure they are consistent with your potty training approach and communicate any special needs or progress.

Suggestions for Ongoing Support and Resources

1. **Stay Informed**
    o **Read Books and Articles:** There are many resources available on potty training. Books and articles can provide additional tips and strategies to support your efforts.
    o **Seek Professional Advice:** If you encounter persistent challenges or have concerns, consider consulting a pediatrician or child psychologist for guidance.
2. **Join Support Groups**

- **Connect with Other Parents:** Join parenting groups or online forums to share experiences and gain support from other parents who are also navigating potty training.
- **Attend Workshops:** Look for local workshops or classes on potty training to learn more and get personalized advice.

3. **Use Potty Training Tools**
   - **Helpful Tools:** Consider using potty training apps, charts, and reward systems to track progress and keep your child motivated.
   - **Progress Charts:** Create or download progress charts to visually track your child's success and provide a tangible reminder of their achievements.

Potty training is a journey that requires patience, consistency, and support. Celebrate each small victory along the way and remember that setbacks are normal. By maintaining a positive attitude and staying consistent with your approach, you will help your child successfully complete this important milestone. Keep reinforcing good habits, celebrate successes, and seek out additional resources and support as needed. Your encouragement and persistence will make the potty training process smoother and more successful for both you and your child.

Chapter 10
Appendices for Potty Training Support

Daily Progress Record

Keeping track of daily progress is essential for understanding how your child is adapting to potty training. A daily progress record allows you to note the time, activity, and success of each potty attempt. This log will help you see patterns, recognize improvements, and identify any challenges that need addressing.

Sample Format:

- **Date:** (e.g., September 3, 2024)
- **Morning Routine:**
    - **Time:** 8:00 AM
    - **Activity:** Woke up, went to the potty
    - **Outcome:** Successful, used the potty
- **Mid-Morning:**
    - **Time:** 10:00 AM
    - **Activity:** Snack time, reminder to use the potty
    - **Outcome:** Attempted, but no success
- **Lunchtime:**

- o **Time:** 12:30 PM
- o **Activity:** After lunch, sat on the potty
- o **Outcome:** Successful, used the potty
- **Afternoon Routine:**
  - o **Time:** 3:00 PM
  - o **Activity:** Played outside, reminded to use the potty before nap
  - o **Outcome:** No attempt, had an accident during nap
- **Evening Routine:**
  - o **Time:** 6:30 PM
  - o **Activity:** Before bath, sat on the potty
  - o **Outcome:** Successful, used the potty
- **Bedtime:**
  - o **Time:** 8:00 PM
  - o **Activity:** Last potty attempt before bed
  - o **Outcome:** Attempted, no success

Notes:

- **Overall Day:** Today was a mix of success and accidents. Morning routines are going well, but the afternoon needs more focus. Consider adjusting nap time reminders.

Weekly Summary Journal

A weekly summary journal provides an overview of your child's potty training journey over the week. This journal helps you assess overall progress, identify recurring issues, and plan for the next week.

Sample Format:

- **Week of:** (e.g., September 1-7, 2024)
- **Overall Progress:**
    - This week showed consistent improvement in morning routines. We had fewer accidents compared to last week, especially in the evenings.
- **Challenges:**
    - Afternoon nap time continues to be a challenge. Accidents are common during this time, and there seems to be some resistance to sitting on the potty.
- **What Worked Well:**
    - Introducing a reward chart has been effective. Stickers for every successful potty attempt motivated our child, particularly during the morning routine.
- **Areas to Improve:**
    - We need to work on reducing accidents during nap time. Perhaps

adding a potty reminder just before nap could help.
- **Plan for Next Week:**
  - Focus on consistent reminders before naps and increasing encouragement through positive reinforcement.
  - Consider setting up a visual timer to help our child understand when it's time to go to the potty.

Reward Survey

Positive reinforcement is a key strategy in potty training. A reward survey allows you to identify what types of rewards motivate your child. This survey should be conducted with your child, making it a fun and interactive process.

Sample Format:

- **Date:** (e.g., September 4, 2024)
- **Favorite Small Rewards:**
  - Stickers: ☐Loved
  - Small Toys: ☐Liked
  - Extra Storytime: ☐Liked
  - Special Snack: ☐Not interested

- **Favorite Big Rewards (For a Week of Success):**
    - Trip to the Park: ☐Loved
    - Movie Night: ☐Liked
    - Playdate with a Friend: ☐Loved
    - New Toy: ☐Liked
- **Notes:**
    - Our child seems to respond best to immediate small rewards like stickers and extra storytime. For larger accomplishments, a trip to the park is the most motivating reward.

Progress Reflection Journal

The progress reflection journal helps you and your child look back on the potty training journey, celebrating successes and learning from challenges. It's a place to express feelings, share experiences, and reflect on how far your child has come.

Sample Format:

- **Date:** (e.g., September 7, 2024)
- **What I'm Proud Of:**
    - I'm proud that I remembered to go to the potty every morning this week. I

didn't have any accidents in the morning, and that makes me feel happy.
- **What Was Hard This Week:**
  - Nap time was hard. I don't like stopping playtime to go to the potty, and I had a few accidents. That made me a little depressed
- **What I Learned:**
  - I learned that going to the potty before my nap helps me stay dry. I also learned that it's okay to have accidents; I just need to try again.
- **My Goals for Next Week:**
  - Next week, I want to remember to go to the potty before my nap so I don't have any accidents. I also want to try to get more stickers for using the potty during the day.
- **Parent's Reflection:**
  - I'm proud of the progress we've made together this week. The morning routine is becoming a habit, and it's great to see our child's confidence growing. We'll continue to work on nap time and keep encouraging with love and patience.

Potty Training Tips Recap

A quick recap of the best potty training tips can serve as a handy reference for you and others involved in your child's training. This section distills the key points of your potty training approach into easy-to-remember advice.

Sample Format:

- **Tip 1:** Stay Consistent - Consistency is key in potty training. Keep the routine predictable so your child knows what to expect.
- **Tip 2:** Positive Reinforcement - Use rewards and praise to motivate your child. No matter how little the accomplishment, acknowledge it.
- **Tip 3:** Be Patient - Potty training is a process, and accidents are part of the journey. Stay calm and supportive.
- **Tip 4:** Listen to Your Child - Pay attention to your child's cues and readiness. Don't rush the process if they're not ready.
- **Tip 5:** Make it Fun - Turn potty training into a fun experience with songs, stories, and a celebratory attitude.

Example Stories of Success

Reading about other families' success stories can inspire and motivate you during the potty training process. These examples provide encouragement and highlight different strategies that have worked for others.

Sample Story 1:

- **Family Name:** The Johnsons
- **Challenge:** Our son was resistant to sitting on the potty, especially during playtime.
- **Solution:** We introduced a "Potty Playtime" game, where he could bring a toy to the bathroom and play while on the potty. This made the experience fun and less stressful.
- **Outcome:** Within two weeks, he was eagerly going to the potty, excited to play with his special potty-time toy.

Sample Story 2:

- **Family Name:** The Smiths
- **Challenge:** Our daughter was having frequent accidents during nap time.
- **Solution:** We started a routine of reading a short book before nap, which included a reminder to use the potty. The quiet time

helped her relax and understand that potty time came before nap time.
- **Outcome:** After a few days, she started going to the potty without a reminder before her nap and stayed dry consistently.

<u>Encouragement Notes</u>

Sometimes, a little encouragement can make all the difference during potty training. Use this section to jot down positive affirmations and notes that can help keep you and your child motivated.

Sample Notes:

- **Note to Myself :** "Any advancement, regardless of size, constitutes progress." Keep going, and remember to be patient with both myself and my child."

- **Note to My Child:** "You're doing an amazing job! I'm so proud of you for trying your best every day. Keep up the great work!"
-
- **Note for Tough Days:** "Some days are harder than others, but that's okay. It's a fresh day to try again tomorrow. We're in this together!"

These appendices provide a solid foundation for supporting potty training in a structured yet flexible way. By keeping detailed records, reflecting on progress, and using positive reinforcement, you can help your child achieve success in their potty training journey. The key is to stay consistent, patient, and encouraging throughout the process.

Printed in Great Britain
by Amazon